*Heroes for Young Readers Activity Guides and audio CDs
are also available. See the back of this book for more information.*

www.HeroesThenAndNow.com

HEROES FOR YOUNG READERS

BETHANY HAMILTON

Riding the Waves

Written by Renee Taft Meloche
Illustrated by Bryan Pollard

YWAM
PUBLISHING

Bethany Hamilton: Riding the Waves   Text © 2014 by Renee Taft Meloche   Illustrations © 2014 by Bryan Pollard
Published by YWAM Publishing, P.O. Box 55787, Seattle, WA 98155   ISBN 978-1-57658-789-8   Printed in China.   All rights reserved.

A tall young girl named Bethany
        loved snorkeling and sun,
and living on an island which
        meant lots of outdoor fun.

Surrounded by the ocean with
        its mighty waves and swells,
she loved to walk along the beach
        collecting pretty shells.

She liked to swim near turtles who
        had made their home the sea,
who glided through the waters and
        were peaceful company.

On this Hawaiian island she
        would hike to waterfalls
or join her older brothers playing
        soccer and paintball.

They sped along the hills where they
        would skateboard up and down.
She kept up with her brothers and
        athletic kids in town.

Of all the sports she really liked,
    the one she loved the most
was catching waves and surfing them
    along the scenic coast.

Her parents also loved to surf
    and taught her what they knew.
Soon Bethany competed and
    she won some contests too.

Then in the year two thousand three,
    when she was just thirteen,
she and her friend Alana went
    to surf on Halloween.

Alana's father Holt and brother
    Byron were nearby.
They all surfed as the sun came out,
    which brightened up the sky.

The water, calm and crystal clear,
    formed waves quite small in size.
The surfers watched and waited for
    a bigger wave to rise.

As Bethany's right hand relaxed
    upon her surfboard's nose,
her left arm dangled in the sea
    until the small waves rose.

But in the distance closing in
    so swift and silently,
a fourteen-foot gray tiger shark
    crept up on Bethany.

She could not see its pointy snout,
    its rolled-back eyes and fins,
its rows of razor-sharp strong teeth
    and rough and armored skin.

She only saw a large gray shape
    approaching her left side.
She did not know it was a shark,
    its huge jaws opened wide.

Its teeth bore down with lightning speed
    and bit into her arm.
Because she felt no pain she did
    not know that she'd been harmed.

In seconds it was over and
　　the gray shark quickly fled
as all the water near her had
　　begun to turn bright red.

A big piece of her surfboard was
　　not there as she held on,
and to her shock she noticed that
　　her whole left arm was gone!

She called out, "Help! A shark bit me
　　and I have been attacked!"
She knew she had to get to shore,
　　a very long way back.

Both Holt and Byron swam to her
    once they had heard her cries.
When they saw what the shark had done,
    they couldn't believe their eyes.

Though Bethany was calm, she said
    with real uncertainty,
"I really can't believe that this
    is happening to me."

As Bethany lay on her board
    the others paddled near.
She knew that she was badly hurt
    and started feeling fear.

Her missing arm was now a stump.
    She needed urgent care.
She had to get to shore and cried,
    "Please, God, help get me there!"

She managed not to panic as
    she lay still while she prayed.
And as she asked God for His help,
    it made her less afraid.

Holt knew he had to wrap her wound
    and did so with his shirt.
He asked her many questions so
    that she would stay alert.

"Now grab my swimming trunks," Holt said.
"The shore is within reach."
Though feeling weak she held on as
he paddled toward the beach.

Alana paddled next to them
with Byron up ahead,
while Bethany pushed doubts away—
"I'm in God's hands," she said.

On shore while Byron phoned for help,
some surfers gathered round.
They wrapped her up with towels on
the soft and sandy ground.

An ambulance was on its way
but taking much too long,
since Bethany was hurting now
and asking for her mom.

Holt drove her toward the hospital
        because of the delay.
As sirens screamed the ambulance
        soon met them on the way.

Two paramedics put her on
        a stretcher in the back.
The ambulance then sped off as
        her world kept going black.

A paramedic held her hand,
        then whispered in her ear.
"Our God will never leave you," he
        said, "nor desert you here."

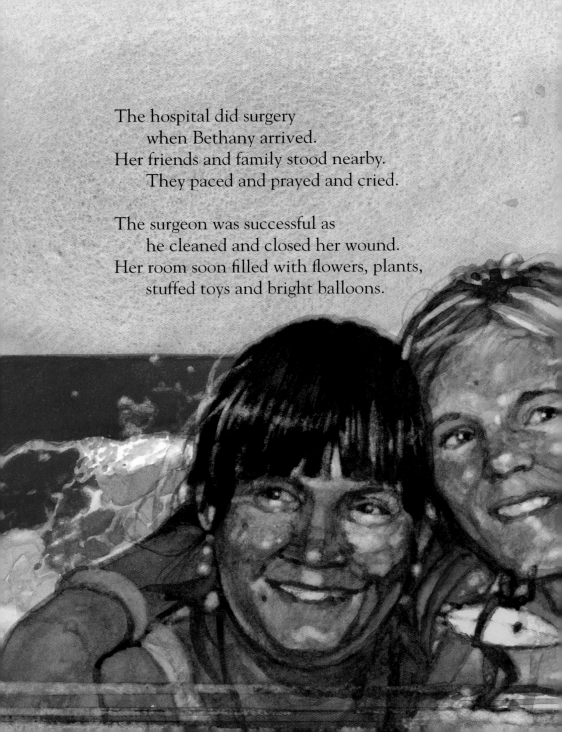

The hospital did surgery
    when Bethany arrived.
Her friends and family stood nearby.
    They paced and prayed and cried.

The surgeon was successful as
    he cleaned and closed her wound.
Her room soon filled with flowers, plants,
    stuffed toys and bright balloons.

She had a lot of visitors
    though she did not feel great.
She saw the sadness in their eyes
    and quickly set them straight.

Although she knew she did not look
    the same way anymore,
she said, "I am the same inside
    and that's what matters more."

As Bethany learned how to dress
    and do things with one hand,
she wondered, *Could I surf again,*
    get on the board and stand?

As people sang and prayed with her,
    it helped her feel less doubt.
She hoped to surf again when all
    her stitches had come out.

But once back home she struggled and
she sometimes just got mad.
A stump replaced her arm now and
it left her feeling bad.

Her parents both encouraged her
and knew she'd find a way
to surf again like she had hoped
before Thanksgiving Day.

Just three weeks after her attack
    she ran across the sand
and splashed into the rolling sea
    to carry out her plan.

Her father, brother and Alana
    also came along.
Her father swimming near her yelled,
    "Go girl!" to cheer her on.

Now Bethany knew shark attacks
    on people are quite rare,
and so she did not worry but
    just felt so happy there.

She focused her attention on
    what she would need to do.
She saw a tall wave rolling in
    as her excitement grew.

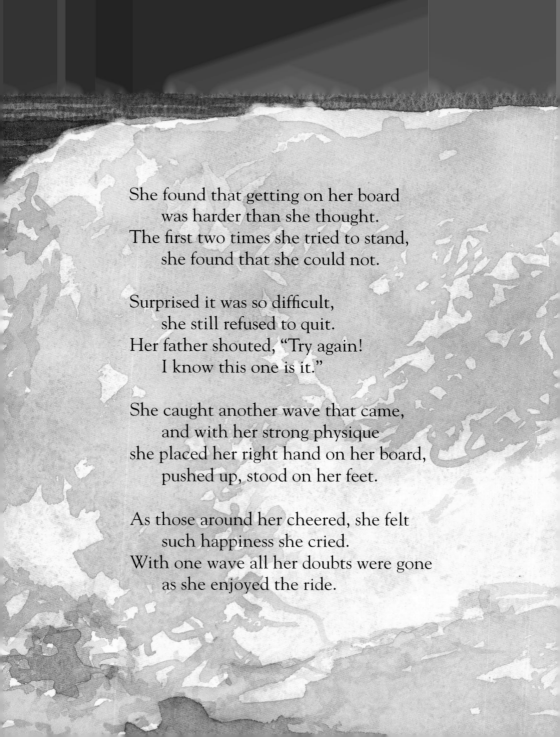

She found that getting on her board
　　was harder than she thought.
The first two times she tried to stand,
　　she found that she could not.

Surprised it was so difficult,
　　she still refused to quit.
Her father shouted, "Try again!
　　I know this one is it."

She caught another wave that came,
　　and with her strong physique
she placed her right hand on her board,
　　pushed up, stood on her feet.

As those around her cheered, she felt
　　such happiness she cried.
With one wave all her doubts were gone
　　as she enjoyed the ride.

Soon surfing got much easier
  as she learned other ways
to paddle, balance and to stand
  throughout the coming days.

Most doubted she'd compete well as
  a one-armed surfing teen,
but nothing would stop Bethany
  from following her dreams.

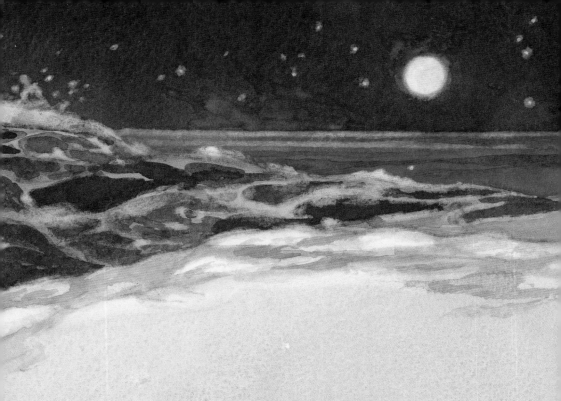

She entered surfing contests and
    competed hard and won
a U.S. surfing championship,
    which she had never done.

She traveled to Australia
    and on that surfing trip
placed second in her age group in
    a big world championship.

Bethany is not content
    to sit and watch the tide.
Her faith has helped her chase away
    the fears she felt inside.

Today she is unstoppable
    and joyful, strong and brave.
She stands up and she surfs the seas
    and rides the biggest waves.

Heroes for Young Readers and Heroes of History for Young Readers are based on the
Christian Heroes: Then & Now and Heroes of History biographies by Janet & Geoff Benge.
Don't miss out on these exciting, true adventures for ages 10 and up!

Christian Heroes: Then & Now

by Janet & Geoff Benge

Adoniram Judson: Bound for Burma
Amy Carmichael: Rescuer of Precious Gems
Betty Greene: Wings to Serve
Brother Andrew: God's Secret Agent
Cameron Townsend: Good News in Every Language
Clarence Jones: Mr. Radio
Corrie ten Boom: Keeper of the Angels' Den
Count Zinzendorf: Firstfruit
C. S. Lewis: Master Storyteller
C. T. Studd: No Retreat
David Bussau: Facing the World Head-on
David Livingstone: Africa's Trailblazer
Dietrich Bonhoeffer: In the Midst of Wickedness
D. L. Moody: Bringing Souls to Christ
Elisabeth Elliot: Joyful Surrender
Eric Liddell: Something Greater Than Gold
Florence Young: Mission Accomplished
Francis Asbury: Circuit Rider
George Müller: The Guardian of Bristol's Orphans
Gladys Aylward: The Adventure of a Lifetime
Hudson Taylor: Deep in the Heart of China
Ida Scudder: Healing Bodies, Touching Hearts
Isobel Kuhn: On the Roof of the World
Jacob DeShazer: Forgive Your Enemies
Jim Elliot: One Great Purpose
John Wesley: The World His Parish
John Williams: Messenger of Peace
Jonathan Goforth: An Open Door in China
Klaus-Dieter John: Hope in the Land of the Incas
Lillian Trasher: The Greatest Wonder in Egypt
Loren Cunningham: Into All the World
Lottie Moon: Giving Her All for China
Mary Slessor: Forward into Calabar

Nate Saint: On a Wing and a Prayer
Paul Brand: Helping Hands
Rachel Saint: A Star in the Jungle
Rowland Bingham: Into Africa's Interior
Samuel Zwemer: The Burden of Arabia
Sundar Singh: Footprints Over the Mountains
Wilfred Grenfell: Fisher of Men
William Booth: Soup, Soap, and Salvation
William Carey: Obliged to Go

Heroes of History
by Janet & Geoff Benge

Abraham Lincoln: A New Birth of Freedom
Alan Shepard: Higher and Faster
Ben Carson: A Chance at Life
Benjamin Franklin: Live Wire
Billy Graham: America's Pastor
Captain John Smith: A Foothold in the New World
Christopher Columbus: Across the Ocean Sea
Clara Barton: Courage under Fire
Daniel Boone: Frontiersman
Davy Crockett: Ever Westward
Douglas MacArthur: What Greater Honor
George Washington: True Patriot
George Washington Carver: From Slave to Scientist
Harriet Tubman: Freedombound
John Adams: Independence Forever
Laura Ingalls Wilder: A Storybook Life
Meriwether Lewis: Off the Edge of the Map
Milton Hershey: More Than Chocolate
Orville Wright: The Flyer
Ronald Reagan: Destiny at His Side
Theodore Roosevelt: An American Original
Thomas Edison: Inspiration and Hard Work
William Penn: Liberty and Justice for All

Available in paperback, e-book, and audiobook formats.
Unit Study Curriculum Guides are available for each biography.